WAS THE BUDDHA A BHIKKHU?

Sangharakshita

Was the Buddha a Bhikkhu?

A Rejoinder to a Reply to *Forty-Three Years Ago*

Windhorse Publications

Published by Windhorse Publications
Unit 1-316 The Custard Factory, Gibb Street, Birmingham, B9 4AA

Printed by The Cromwell Press,
Melksham, Wiltshire.

Cover design: Dhammarati

The cover shows a drum slab, Amaravati Stupa, 1st century BCE
Courtesy of the Trustees of the British Museum

British Library Cataloguing in Publication Data:
A catalogue record for this book is available from the British Library.

ISBN 0 904766 71 3

Preface

WHEN SANGHARAKSHITA DISCOVERED that his higher ordination had been compromised by the presence in the ordaining chapter of an 'impure' monk and that, technically speaking, he was therefore not a bhikkhu, he could have kept the discovery to himself. The offending monk's blemish was hardly a matter of common knowledge, and there were probably few people around able to remember who had actually taken part in the ceremony! Surely, what really mattered was that Sangharakshita had wanted to become a bhikkhu; he had undergone the ordination ceremony; he was now living as a bhikkhu, and was widely accepted as one. Common sense too must have suggested that Sangharakshita was hardly the first bhikkhu to find himself in this position. Why make a fuss?

For long time, then, Sangharakshita kept things to himself. But he did not forget, and as the years went by the implications of his discovery prompted a series of reflections that were little less than revolutionary. These reflections have borne decisively on his vision of the Buddhist spiritual life and are responsible for several radical features of the Western Buddhist Order (WBO) and the Friends of the Western Buddhist Order (FWBO) which he founded in the late sixties. They also inform much of his literary output, not least a booklet entitled *Forty-Three Years Ago: Reflections on my Bhikkhu Ordination, on the Occasion of the Twenty-Fifth Anniversary of the Western Buddhist Order*, published in 1993, in which he outlined some of the reflections that had occupied his mind for four decades.

Was it conceivable, he wondered, that the entire Theravāda ordination tradition fell short of the strict technical requirements laid down by the Vinaya—or at least could not be proved not to? If so, did this not raise searching questions about personal and collective religious life in the Theravāda world, given the extent to which it revolved more around the technical fact of the bhikkhu's status than it did around less formal but more directly spiritual concerns? Was it not time to reaffirm the value of 'Sūtra-style' monasticism—a full time spiritual life defined by commitment and practice rather than technical status, and to recognize, even, that a 'bad' monk might be the better Buddhist than a good one? Along the way, such reflections and questions inevitably sprouted more: what is one really doing when one venerates the robe? What effect does the laity's unquestioning reverence have on the spiritual health of a bhikkhu? Do women need to resurrect the bhikkhunī sangha in order to live spiritual lives?

Such questions and comments expressed the sometimes painfully won insights of a man who had been willing to traverse India on foot in order to receive ordination within the Theravāda tradition, and whose life ever since has been vigorously dedicated to the practice and teaching of the

Buddha-Dharma. These were the questions and insights, too, that had led Sangharakshita to found a new Buddhist Order whose male and female members were neither monks and nuns *nor* laymen, and for whom life-style, while crucial as an *expression* of commitment, did not submerge or obscure the crucial *priority* of commitment—or in traditional Buddhist terminology, one's Going for Refuge to the Three Jewels.

Of course I am partisan, but am I hopelessly partisan? Am I right in supposing that those sixty or so pages should have provoked a spirited round of discussion and debate throughout the Buddhist world? Perhaps they still will. Meanwhile, a year on, the sole published response seems to have been that of Bhikkhu Brahmavamso in the Forest Hermitage *Newsletter*. It is Sangharakshita's reply to Brahmavamso that you have before you.

At first sight, these pages offer an encounter with Sangharakshita in 'fine-detail mode'. His earlier paper's significance has been publicly challenged on the grounds that his 'Reflections', being based on a flawed understanding of the Vinaya, are technically unsound. Inevitably, Sangharakshita feels required to establish, publicly, that they were not. He does this, not out of any desire to assert an expertise with regard to the Vinaya—of which he freely admits a lack, but because a distracting and unnecessary obstruction has been placed in the way of ideas he would like to see shared and discussed. The obstruction must be cleared away.

It is a task that has been thrust upon him. It is too, as you will see, a task which involves a lot of hard work—little of which offered him the pleasure of developing the substantive dimensions of his previous work. But perform it he does, with meticulous, painstaking care and attention. How many of us, I wonder, might have read Brahmavamso's article, contemplated the nature of the work involved in a suitable answer, and quietly shrugged it off as a small article in a small magazine by a relatively unknown bhikkhu?

Perhaps it says a lot about both men, and about their experience of Buddhism, that Brahmavamso feels impelled to defuse a perceived attack on the importance of Theravāda technicalities while Sangharakshita feels perhaps even more strongly impelled to see off the challenge so as to redirect his readers' attention to the wider and deeper issues—most of which Brahmavamso has significantly ignored.

In *Forty-Three Years Ago*, when Sangharakshita distinguishes between 'Vinaya-style' and 'Sūtra-style' monasticism, he effectively draws a distinction between two approaches to the spiritual life itself. To the extent that the two men can be seen to embody these approaches, then this living record of their encounter vividly illustrates—and so returns us to—the very heart of the issues raised in that earlier book.

Nagabodhi
Vimalakula Community
July 1994

WAS THE BUDDHA A BHIKKHU?

A FRIEND TO WHOM I HAD WRITTEN about his new book replied
that he greatly appreciated my recognition of the book's
value, adding, 'As you may have found yourself, publication
is often followed by a disquieting silence.' I had indeed
found that this was often the case. But not always. Publication, I had also found, was sometimes followed by a definite
response. This has certainly been the case with *Forty-Three
Years Ago*, subtitled 'Reflections on my Bhikkhu Ordination,
on the Occasion of the Twenty-Fifth Anniversary of the
Western Buddhist Order', which was published a year ago.
The response to this little work has not been deafening, but
there has certainly been a response, and with the exception
of a single dissentient voice it has been welcoming and
appreciative. One Buddhist correspondent—*not* a member
of the FWBO—wrote to say that he found himself in agreement with more or less everything I said about the am-
biguous status of the bhikkhu ordination. 'In a sense the
whole issue is blindingly self-evident,' he concluded. 'As
you point out, though, it is concealed by a huge conspiracy

of Asian (and non-Asian) face-saving self-interest.' While agreement with what one says may be more pleasant, disagreement is often more useful. I shall therefore make no further reference to the welcoming and appreciative response that *Forty-Three Years Ago* has received, but concentrate, instead, on the criticisms of the single dissentient voice.

This dissentient voice made itself heard in the pages of the April 1994 issue of the Forest Hermitage *Newsletter*, edited by Phra Ajahn Khemadhammo from Wat Pah Santidhamma, Lower Fulbrook, nr Sherbourne, Warwick. The voice is not that of Phra Ajahn Khemadhammo himself. It is that of Bhikkhu Brahmavamso, of the Bodhinyana Monastery, Perth, Australia. 'While I was in Australia in January,' Ajahn Khemadhammo tells us in his editorial article, 'I discussed a certain booklet with my friend Phra Ajahn Brahmavamso and later I sent him a copy. About a month ago the fax machine disgorged a detailed, handwritten, three page response, with a note allowing me to edit it. In the interests of space, what appears in the next column and over the page has been much hacked about and is minus the references. The original could be made available on request.' Having thus handed over the responsibility for replying to my booklet to his friend Brahmavamso, Khemadhammo turns to the more congenial business of telling his readers about the 'vastly improved car park and drive' his hermitage is soon to have.

Naturally I read the shortened version of Bhikkhu Brahmavamso's article with interest, and before long was able to lay my hands on a copy of the original, unedited version. (Strange to say, the April issue of the Forest Hermitage *Newsletter* never reached the Order Office, though hitherto it had been received there regularly.) Whereas the shortened version is entitled 'On the Validity of the Bhikkhu Ordination in Theravada,' the original is entitled 'On the Validity and Meaning of the Bhikkhu Ordination in Theravada.' Unlike his friend Khemadhammo, Brahmavamso does not hesitate to mention either the title of the offending booklet or the name of the author. 'A recently published booklet "Forty-Three Years Ago",' he writes, 'written by Sangharakshita, questions the validity and meaning of the bhikkhu ordination in Theravada.' Of course I do very much more than that. The booklet deals with a number of topics; but obviously only one of them is of any interest to Brahmavamso.

'Basing his argument on his own bhikkhu ordination in India in 1950, Sangharakshita comes to the conclusion that "All this goes to show that technically valid ordination (as a bhikkhu) is virtually impossible of attainment and that if one did, miraculously, obtain it, one could not know that one had done so."(p.23).' This is not quite correct. My argument that technically valid ordination is virtually impossible of attainment and that if one did, miraculously, obtain it, one could not know that one had done so, is not based on my own ordination, i.e. not based simply on the fact that one member of the ordaining chapter was not really a bhikkhu. As the preceding pages made clear, it is based mainly on the difficulty of knowing (i) whether all those conferring the ordination were really bhikkhus (i.e. had been validly ordained by bhikkhus who had themselves been validly ordained—and so on back to the beginnings of the coenobitical Monastic Order) and (ii) whether the ordination ceremony itself had been conducted in strict accordance with the requirements of the Vinaya. My own ordination, or rather my discovery that not all those taking part in it were really bhikkhus, was the starting point of a series of reflections, not the first link in a chain of logical deductions, and my argument would still hold good even if all those taking part in my ordination had been really bhikkhus—not that I could actually have known this to be the case. Brahmavamso appears not to see this, and therefore continues, 'The misleading allegation that the bhikkhu ordination is practically invalid is so serious a charge that it deserves a serious reply,' as though I had come to the conclusion that bhikkhu ordination was technically invalid only on the basis of my own experience of ordination in India in 1950.

The allegation that bhikkhu ordination is practically invalid (I am assuming that Brahmavamso's 'practically' is equivalent to my 'technically') is indeed a serious one, especially in the eyes of those who are accustomed to think of their spiritual life, and their privileged status within the Buddhist community, as being dependent on their having been ordained in the technical Vinaya sense. It therefore is not astonishing that Brahmavamso should have considered my allegation, as he terms it, deserving of a serious reply. I appreciate his willingness to engage in dialogue in this way and only wish his reply could have been even more serious and have embraced some of the more fundamental topics— more fundamental than the question of the technical validity of bhikkhu ordination—dealt with in *Forty-Three Years Ago*.

He begins by going straight to what he sees as the main point.

Unfortunately, Sangharakshita, though strong in many other areas of Buddhist scholarship, has only a limited understanding of the bhikkhu's Vinaya. His argument against the validity of the bhikkhu ordination crumbles because of a mistaken premise. On pages 8 and 9, he assumes his own bhikkhu ordination was invalid because of the presence of a 'sham monk', that is a layman in the guise of a bhikkhu. One of the members of the assembly, Sangharakshita later discovered, had committed a Parajika (an offence entailing immediate and automatic return to the status of layman), had not yet owned up to the fault, and was thus technically a layman in the robes of a monk.

Whether I am strong in other areas of Buddhist scholarship is not for me to say, but I can freely confess that my understanding of the bhikkhu's Vinaya is (and was) a limited one. Few bhikkhus have more than a limited understanding of the Vinaya, which is probably why Khemadhammo had to go half way round the world to find someone who could attempt to reply (in English) to my charge that the bhikkhu ordination is technically invalid. Far from consisting of a few simple rules, the Vinaya (i.e. the Vinaya-Piṭaka) is a complex and elaborate body of monastic law that occupies, in the English translation, six very substantial volumes, mastery of which, together with the extensive commentarial literature, is the work of half a lifetime of scholarly specialization. The average Theravādin bhikkhu probably has no more understanding of the Vinaya *in this sense* than the average law-abiding English citizen has of Blackstone's *Commentaries on the Laws of England*. Such understanding of it as he possesses he acquires by participating in the life of the monastic community, doing what other monks do, and not doing what they do not do. Thus he does not *know* that he is observing the Vinaya (in order to know this he would have to be personally acquainted with the appropriate texts); he only believes that he is observing it, and he is able to believe that he is observing it because he believes that there are monks who do know the Vinaya. Once again, spiritual life is based on belief rather than on knowledge, in this case not just on belief that one is a bhikkhu, in the technical Vinaya sense, but on belief that one is observing the Vinaya. As I point out in *Forty-Three Years Ago,*[1] belief of this kind is not a very secure foundation for the spiritual life. But perhaps there is no need for me to enlarge on this topic in the present connection. Brahmavamso continues:

> According to the Vinaya, the third of the Tipitaka dealing with the monastic rules and procedures, the assumption that the presence of a 'sham monk' invalidates the ordination ceremony is certainly wrong. There may be several 'sham monks' in the assembly conferring the bhikkhu status on a candidate, but as long as there are at least five bhikkhus (ten in the Ganges Valley of India) also present, then the ordination is valid (see Pali Text Society's 'Vinaya Pitakam', vol 1, p 319f; Mahavagga, chapter 9, vs 4.1–4.4.)

Since Brahmavamso does not actually quote the passage to which he refers (Khemadhammo's shortened version does not even give the references, leaving the reader to take it on trust that the purport of the passage is as claimed), let me quote it in full. Before so doing, however, there is an ambiguity to be cleared up. In speaking of my ordination I did not distinguish, as perhaps I should have done, between what I called the ordaining chapter (Brahmavamso's 'assembly') and the quorum required for ordination in the Middle Country. My ordination was invalid not so much because there was a single 'sham monk' in the ordaining chapter as because the number of 'sham monks' (as I afterwards discovered them to be) in that chapter was such as to render it inquorate for the purpose of bhikkhu ordination. That such was the case should be evident from my comment that most of the bhikkhus taking part in my ordination were *'like the bhikkhu with a wife and son*, bad monks' (my present italics).[2] Now for the promised quotation from the Vinaya-Piṭaka.

'If, monks, a fourfold Order, carrying out a (formal) act, should carry out the (formal) act with a nun as the fourth (member), then it is not a (formal) act and ought not to be carried out. If, monks, a fourfold Order, carrying out a (formal) act, should carry out the (formal) act with a probationer as the fourth (member) ... with a novice ... with a woman novice ... with a disavower of the training ... with one who has committed an extreme offence ... with one who is suspended for not seeing an offence ... with one who is suspended for not making amends for an offence ... with one who is suspended for not giving up a wrong view ... with a eunuch ... with one living in communion as it were by theft ... with one who has gone over to a sect ... with an animal ... with a matricide ... with a parricide ... with a slayer of ones perfected ... with a seducer of a nun ... with a schismatic ... with a shedder of (a tathagata's) blood ... with a hermaphrodite ... with one belonging to a different communion ... with one staying in a different

boundary ... with one standing above the ground by
psychic potency ... with one against whom an Order is
carrying out a (formal) act as the fourth (member), it is
not a (formal) act and ought not to be carried out.'
Carrying out by a Fourfold (Order).

'If, monks, a fivefold Order, carrying out a (formal)
act, should carry out the (formal) act with a nun as the
fifth (member) ... with one against whom the Order is
carrying out a (formal) act as the fifth (member), it is not
a (formal) act and ought not to be carried out.'
Carrying out by a Fivefold (Order).

'If, monks, a tenfold Order, carrying out a (formal) act,
should carry out the (formal) act with a nun as the tenth
(member) ... with one against whom the Order is
carrying out a (formal) act as the tenth (member), it is
not a (formal) act and ought not to be carried out.'
Carrying out by a Tenfold (Order).[3]

The first thing that strikes one about this passage (apart from
its legalistic character) is that it does not support Brahmavamso's contention that there may be several 'sham monks'
in the assembly conferring the bhikkhu ordination on a
candidate. What it actually says, with regard to the carrying
out of a (formal) act (such as ordination), by an Order of four,
or five, or ten bhikkhus, is that such a (formal) act is not a
(formal) act (i.e. is invalid) if the fourth, or fifth, or tenth
member of the Order, as the case may be, is a nun ... down
to one against whom an Order is carrying out a (formal) act.
It says nothing about the presence of 'sham monks' in the
assembly, as distinct from their (disallowed) membership of
the quorum. The clear purport of the passage is to exclude

'sham monks' from the quorum, *not* to permit their presence in the assembly at the time of ordination or other (formal) acts of the Order. Why it is important to Brahmavamso, as apparently to the tradition to which he belongs, that the presence of 'sham monks' should not invalidate the ordination ceremony, as long as there are at least five bhikkhus, i.e. bhikkhus who are not 'sham monks', (ten in the Ganges Valley) also present, will transpire later. Meanwhile, by way of contrast to the passage from the Vinaya Piṭaka, let me quote a passage about the 'monastic' life from the Sutta-Piṭaka.

Good is restraint of sight. Good is restraint of hearing. Good is restraint of smell. Good is restraint of taste.

Good is restraint in deed. Good is restraint in word. Good is restraint in thought. Good is restraint everywhere. The monk restrained in every way is freed from all suffering.

He who is controlled in hand, foot, speech, and thought; he who delights in meditation, composed, solitary and contented,—him they call a monk.

That monk who is controlled in tongue, moderate in speech, is not puffed up, who explains the meaning and the text,—sweet, indeed, is his speech.

Abiding in the Teaching, delighting in the Teaching, pondering over the Teaching, calling to mind the Teaching,—a monk such as this does not fall away from the Teaching.

A monk should not despise what he has received, and look with envy upon the gain of others. The monk who envies the gains of others does not attain concentration.

Even if a monk's gain be slight, yet let him not despise it. If pure of life and unremitting in effort, he is praised by the very gods.

He who nowhere in the mind and body finds aught of which to say 'This is mine', he who grieves not for that which he has not,—he indeed is called a monk.

The monk who abides in loving-kindness, whose joy is in the Teaching of the Buddha,—that monk attains the peace of *Nibbāna*, the quiet happy ending of compounded existence.

Empty this boat, O monk; emptied, it will go lightly with you. Cutting out lust and hatred, you will thereby go to *Nibbāna*.

Cut away these five: (self-illusion, doubt, indulgence in rites and ceremonies, lust and ill will). Abandon these five: (desire for life in worlds of form, craving for formless realms, pride, restlessness of mind, and ignorance). Cultivate these five: (confidence, energy, recollectedness, meditation, and wisdom). The monk who has gone beyond the five fetters is called 'Crossed-the-flood'.

Meditate, O monk; do not be heedless. Do not let your mind revolve around sensual pleasures. Do not, through negligence, swallow a ball of (red hot) iron. As you are burnt, do not cry 'O what torture'.

There is no concentration for him who lacks wisdom; nor is there wisdom for him who lacks concentration. In whom are found both concentration and wisdom,—he, indeed, is in the presence of *Nibbāna*.

To the monk who has retired to a lonely abode, who has calmed his mind, who clearly perceives the

Teaching,—to him there arises a joy transcending that of men.

Whenever he reflects on the rise and fall of aggregates, he assuredly experiences joy and happiness. To the discerning, this is as nectar.

For the wise monk, these are the first things to cultivate: sense-control, contentment, restraint through observance of the rules of discipline, association with noble and energetic friends whose livelihood is pure.

Let the monk be hospitable, refined in conduct; full of joy he will thereby make an end of suffering.

Just as the jasmine sheds its withered flowers, so, O monks, you should totally shed lust and hatred.

The monk who is calm in body (or subdued in deed), calm in speech, calm in mind, well composed, emptied of all appetite for the world,—such a one is called 'Tranquillised'.

By thyself rouse (or censure) thyself; thyself examine thyself. Thus self-guided, mindful, the monk shall dwell in happiness.

Oneself is one's own protector; oneself is one's own refuge. Control, therefore, your own self as a merchant, a spirited charger.

Full of joy, full of faith in the Teaching of the Buddha, the monk will attain the Peaceful State, the happy stilling of the compounds of existence.

Even a young monk who devotes himself to the Teaching of the Buddha, illumines this world as does the moon freed from a cloud.[4]

In these two passages, one from the Vinaya-Piṭaka and one from the Sutta-Piṭaka, we breathe two different atmospheres, even find ourselves in two different worlds. One is the world of individual spiritual life; the other the world of highly organized corporate (coenobitical) existence. In one the emphasis is on the realization of principles; in the other, conformity to rules. Not that the two are mutually exclusive *in toto*. One of the *Dhammapada* verses speaks of the wise monk as cultivating restraint through observance of the rules of discipline (*pāṭimokkha*), while the Vinaya passage's reference to a disavower of the training (*sikkhā*) implies the existence of an (ethical and spiritual) training to be disavowed. Nonetheless the distance between the two worlds is immense. There lies between them a process of development that extended over many decades, probably over two or three centuries, and that of course continued well beyond the Buddha's own lifetime. This process has been little studied, and so far as I know S. Dutt's *Early Buddhist Monachism* (1924) represents the only systematic attempt to apply the methods of the higher criticism to the Vinaya literature, as distinct from merely describing that literature. Indeed, since the pioneering work of C.A.F. Rhys Davids and G.C. Pande there has been little (in English, at least) in the way of application of the higher criticism to the literature of the Sutta-Piṭaka either. That application in its full rigour is still to come, and no doubt will affect our understanding of Early Buddhism in much the same way that the work of such figures as Eichhorn, Strauss, and Renan in the last century and Schweitzer in the first half of this century affected our understanding of the Bible and Early Christianity. However, I am digressing. The fact that the Vinaya is not a unitary (originally oral) composition, with a single author, the Buddha, formed no part of my argument in *Forty-Three Years Ago*, though it could well have done, and I advert to it now because the assumption that the Vinaya is a unitary composition, the author of which is the Buddha, appears to underlie Brahmavamso's 'fundamentalist' attitude to bhikkhu ordination and needs, therefore, to be borne in mind. The contrast between the world of individual spiritual life, as represented by the *Dhammapada* verses, and that of highly organized coenobitical monasticism, as represented by the passage from the Mahāvagga of the Vinaya-Piṭaka, also serves to illustrate what I meant when, in *Forty-Three Years Ago*,[5] I expressed a wish to see a revival, throughout the Buddhist world, of what I termed Sūtra-style monasticism—not of Vinaya-style monasticism. But to return to Brahmavamso and his article. Having, as he (wrongly) believes, shown that according to the Vinaya—at least according to the Mahāvagga passage to which he refers—there may be several 'sham monks' in the assembly conferring the bhikkhu ordination on a candidate, he continues:

> The bhikkhus included in the quorum do not need to be 'parisuddha or completely pure' as Sangharakshita mistakenly stated on p.9. They just need to be bhikkhus, not laymen, and not under suspension imposed by the extremely rare act of the Sangha called UKKHEPANIYA-KAMMA (see Pali Text Society's 'Vinaya Pitakam', vol 2, p 21–28; Cullavagga, chapter 1, vs 25–35).

From the way the reference is given one would naturally think that Cullavagga 1 vs 25–35 contained a straightforward and unambiguous statement to the effect that the bhikkhus included in the quorum do not need to be completely pure. But such is not the case. In fact it deals, in a highly legalistic manner, and for ten whole pages together, with the procedures to be followed with regard to a monk who, having fallen into an offence, does not want to see the offence (as an offence). (*To begin with*, there are the Forty-Three Observances connected with a (Formal) Act of Suspension for Not Seeing an Offence.) Opinions differ regarding what constitutes 'complete purity', both within the scholarly community and among bhikkhus. I have participated in at least one bhikkhu ordination, presided over by a very distinguished Sinhalese mahāthera (he may have had only a limited understanding of the Vinaya), prior to which we all 'confessed our sins' and purified ourselves—presumably so as to ensure that we conferred the ordination in a state of (complete?) purity. The bhikkhus whose presence within the sīmā at my own ordination rendered the assembly inquorate for the purpose of ordination, and my ordination therefore invalid, were certainly not 'completely pure' in the sense of not being pārājita. But Brahmavamso is determined to pursue the question of quorum to the bitter end.

> Even if a bhikkhu has committed a gross offence such as Sanghadisesa, a group of offences next in severity to the Parajika; such as for lustfully embracing a woman for example, then he may still make up the quorum for the ordination ceremony (Pali Text Society's 'Vinaya Pitakam', vol 1, p 319f; Mahavagga, chapter 9, vs 4.1–4.4). Even if the preceptor (the UPAJJHAYA) is not really a bhikkhu but a layman appearing as a monk, then this still does not invalidate the ordination (Buddhaghosa's Vinaya Commentary, the Samantapasadika, Pali Text Society's edition, vol 14, p 868). A bhikkhu ordination only fails

for 'lack of a quorum' (PARISA-VIPATTI) when there are less than five bhikkhus (ten in the Ganges Valley) among the assembly conferring the ordination. Sangharakshita does not say how many were present at his ordination ceremony in India in 1950, but if for example there were thirteen of which only three were later discovered not to have been bhikkhus, then his ordination would be valid and he would have been a bhikkhu.

As I have already explained, the number of 'sham monks' present at my ordination was sufficient to render it inquorate for the purpose of bhikkhu ordination, and although I appreciate Brahmavamso's openness to the possibility that I may have been validly ordained my ordination must therefore remain technically invalid and I must be content to be living, now, as a Sūtra-style monk rather than as a Vinaya-style bhikkhu. In any case, even though I came to know that some of the bhikkhus present at my ordination were really laymen appearing as monks, of the remainder (with one exception) I never knew that they were *not* laymen appearing as monks. Hence there was really never any question of my *knowing* that I was a bhikkhu in the technical Vinaya sense. I only believed myself to be such—mistakenly, as it turned out. The Mahāvagga passage to which Brahmavamso refers in support of his contention that a bhikkhu who has committed a gross offence such as Sanghādisesa may still make up the quorum for the ordination ceremony is the very passage to which he referred, earlier on, in support of his contention that there may be 'sham monks' in the assembly conferring ordination on a candidate. But again the passage does not support his contention. There is no straightforward and unambiguous statement to the effect that a bhikkhu who has committed a gross offence such as Saṅghādisesa may still make up the quorum for the ordination ceremony. At best this can only be inferred from the fact that a bhikkhu who has committed a grave offence is not explicitly mentioned among the twenty-four kinds of person with whom as a fourth, or a fifth, or a tenth member a (formal) act of the Sangha may not be carried out. But even if the passage in question is accepted as supporting Brahmavamso's contention, and if both 'sham monks' and monks who have committed a gross offence may be present in the assembly conferring ordination on a candidate, and even make up the quorum, this logically results in a very strange situation, as we shall see. The assertion by Buddhaghosa, who lived a thousand years after the Buddha, that a bhikkhu ordination is not invalid even if the upajjhāya or preceptor is not really a bhikkhu but a layman appearing as a monk is on a par with his assertion that even if a bhikkhu has twenty meals a day, provided they are all taken before midday he is still a 'one-mealer'. Both assertions represent a *reductio ad absurdum* of the kind of legalistic understanding of the Vinaya to which Brahmavamso would seem to be committed.

From my ordination ceremony in India in 1950 Brahma-vamso turns to his own nine years as a bhikkhu in Thailand.

Sangharakshita then proceeds from his mistaken premise to question the validity of every bhikkhu ordination. Even if his own bhikkhu ordination in India does not turn out to be valid because there were not the required ten bhikkhus present, it is quite illogical to infer that all bhikkhu ordinations are invalid. Theravada Buddhism in 1950's India is hardly representative of the Theravada Buddhist World as a whole! In Thailand, where I spent nine years as a bhikkhu, bhikkhu ordinations require only five bhikkhus to complete the quorum, but usually there are at least twenty present, sometimes over a hundred. Among the many tens of thousands of monks in Thailand there will of course be some 'sham monks' who have committed a Parajika and not owned up, but the vast majority would not have committed a Parajika and would be bona-fide bhikkhus who can be counted to make up the quorum. One does not need a degree in statistical analysis to appreciate that, given the numbers usually attending a bhikkhu ordination in Thailand this century and considering the number of 'sham monks' as a percentage of the whole Bhikkhu Sangha, it is extremely unlikely that a bhikkhu ordination can fail for lack of a quorum.

In *Forty-Three Years Ago* I certainly do not infer that all bhikkhu ordinations are invalid from the invalidity of my own ordination. Such an inference would indeed be quite illogical, and I am astonished that Brahmavamso should be disingenuous enough to credit me with it. As I have more than once made clear, my argument that technically valid ordination is virtually impossible of attainment and that if one did, miraculously, obtain it, one could not know that one had done so, is not based on my own ordination, but on the difficulty of knowing (i) whether all those conferring the ordination were really bhikkhus and (ii) whether the ordination ceremony itself had been conducted in strict accordance with the requirements of the Vinaya. My discovery that not all those taking part in my ordination were really bhikkhus was (to repeat myself) the starting point of a series of reflections, not the first link in a chain of deductions. It alerted me to the fact that a bhikkhu ordination *could* be seriously flawed, i.e. could be technically invalid, despite the sincerity of the candidate, and led me, eventually, to consider the likelihood of all bhikkhu ordinations being seriously flawed and the reasons for this being the case. If I proceeded from any premise, and if there was any logical inference, it was as follows: (i) In order to know that I was validly ordained and that I am, therefore, technically a real bhikkhu, I must know whether the assembly ordaining me includes a quorum of validly ordained, real bhikkhus. (ii) I cannot know whether the assembly ordaining me includes a quorum of validly ordained, real bhikkhus, because in order to know them to be such I would have to know all their predecessors in monastic ordination to have been such, and obviously I cannot know this. (iii) Therefore I cannot know that I was validly ordained and that I am, therefore, technically a real bhikkhu. All this has important implications for legalistic, Vinaya-style monasticism. As I point out in *Forty-Three Years Ago*,[6] if a bhikkhu's spiritual life depends on ordination, and if he does not know, even cannot know, whether he is really ordained, then his spiritual life—not to mention his socioreligious status—has a very insecure foundation. In fact it has no foundation, and if it is to have a real foundation then that foundation must be located in his observance of the sikkhāpadas and other ethical and spiritual practices of Sūtra-style monasticism. (Not that Vinaya-style monastics do not observe the sikkhāpadas. They often do; but in their case spiritual life is not *based* on such observance. It is based on their belief that they have been validly ordained and are bhikkhus in the technical Vinaya sense.) As for Theravāda

Buddhism in the India of the 1950s not being representative of the Theravāda Buddhist world, no doubt it was not—to its advantage in some ways. It was certainly not representative of 1950s Theravāda Buddhist Ceylon (as Sri Lanka was then known), where a bhikkhu assassinated the prime minister, any more than it was representative, in the 1970s, of a Theravāda Buddhist Thailand where bhikkhus blessed tanks and guns and where Kittivaddho, the famous charismatic preacher, told mass audiences that it was no more a sin to kill a Communist than to kill a fish or a fowl to offer to a monk. Glittering golden spires, however beautiful, and royal or presidential patronage, however splendid, are not very reliable indicators of the spiritual health of a religion.

Nor, for the matter of that, does the number of those in yellow (or even in brown) robes constitute any such indicator. In Thailand, Brahmavamso reminds us, there are many tens of thousands of monks, and some of these, he admits, will be 'sham monks' who have committed a pārājika and not owned up, but the vast majority would not have committed a pārājika and would be bona fide bhikkhus who could be counted to make up the quorum. What he overlooks is the fact that it is not sufficient for the five bhikkhus completing the quorum not to have committed a pārājika. If they are to confer a valid ordination it is also necessary that they should have been validly ordained themselves, in the technical Vinaya sense, and that the bhikkhus making up the quorum that ordained *them* should have been validly ordained, and so on back to the very beginning of the coenobitical Monastic Order. Logically speaking, as I point out in *Forty-Three Years Ago*,[7] and should not really have to point out again, one can be sure that any bhikkhu was validly ordained only if one can be sure that all his predecessors in monastic ordination were validly ordained. Brahmavamso also overlooks the fact that, as I also point out, an ordination, to be valid, has not only to be performed by bhikkhus who have not committed a pārājika, and who have themselves been validly ordained; it has also to be performed in strict accordance with the requirements of the Vinaya, mistakes in meeting which can easily occur. Perhaps one needs a degree in statistical analysis after all, even given the numbers usually attending a bhikkhu ordination in Thailand this century, for one has to take into consideration not only the number of 'sham monks' as a percentage of the whole Bhikkhu Sangha, but also the percentage of invalid ordinations in the past, whether due to incomplete quorum, wrong procedure, or any other reason. Far from it being extremely unlikely that a bhikkhu ordination can fail for lack of a quorum, it seems extremely unlikely that it should *not* fail. Brahmavamso himself, perhaps inadvertently, only claims that such a failure is *unlikely* to occur. But unlikelihood is a very different thing from certainty, and the unlikelihood of there not being a quorum at one's ordination, and hence of one not really being a bhikkhu, in the technical Vinaya sense, is not a very secure foundation for a spiritual life based, as a bhikkhu's spiritual life purports to be based, on a technically valid ordination.

Yet even assuming that one does not need a degree in statistical analysis and that, as Brahmavamso evidently believes, given the numbers usually attending a bhikkhu ordination in Thailand this century and considering the number of 'sham monks' as a percentage of the whole Bhikkhu Sangha, it is extremely unlikely that a bhikkhu ordination can fail for lack of a quorum, where does this in fact leave him? It leaves him in the strange situation to which I alluded earlier. Let us try to get the situation more clearly into view. Brahmavamso maintains that the presence of 'sham monks' in the assembly does not invalidate a bhikkhu ordination. He also maintains, following Buddhaghosa, that even if the preceptor is not really a bhikkhu but a layman appearing as a monk, possibly because he has committed a pārājika, then this still does not invalidate the ordination. Thus he asks us to envisage a situation in which a hundred monks, let us say, assemble in the sīmā for an ordination ceremony. An indeterminate number of them (Brahmavamso says 'several', but in view of the difficulty of knowing whether a bhikkhu's predecessors in ordination were validly ordained this should surely be 'the majority' or even 'all') are, admittedly, 'sham monks', or laymen appearing as monks. How do we tell the 'sham monks' from the real monks? Do the former sit apart from the latter, for example? Apparently they do not. They are all mixed up together in the sīmā and we have no means of telling which are which. We do not have any means of telling whether the upajjhāya or preceptor is a 'sham monk' or a real monk—or the ācariya or instructor, or the first, or the second, or the third kammavācā bhikkhus. (Incidentally, if the upajjhāya or preceptor may be a layman appearing as a monk, as Brahmavamso maintains, then in theory at least he may be a layman appearing as a layman.)[8] Brahmavamso then asks us to envisage a situation—and this is the principal reason for its strangeness—in which the candidate presenting himself for ordination does not really know what percentage, if any, of the bhikkhus in the assembly are 'sham monks', whether the preceptor is a layman appearing as a monk, or whether the bhikkhus playing an active part in the ordination ceremony are really monks. In other words the candidate cannot know if he has been validly ordained and that he is, by virtue of that ordination, a bhikkhu in the technical Vinaya sense. He can only *hope* that he has been ordained, and is a real monk, on the grounds of its being—according to Brahmavamso—*unlikely* that there are not, scattered among the hundred monks assembled for the ceremony, five bona fide monks who can be counted to make up the quorum. Formalism could hardly go farther than this! Surely it would be better to abandon the charade of technically valid ordination and base bhikkhu status (if there is to be such a thing) simply on the observance of the relevant sikkhāpadas. But it is doubtful if Brahmavamso, wedded as he is to the concept of a technically valid bhikkhu ordination, would be willing to do this. Monastic life is for him unthinkable apart from technically valid bhikkhu ordination, which is why he is prepared to defend such ordination at all costs and why it is important to him, as to the tradition to which he belongs, that the presence of 'sham monks' in the assembly at the time of ordination should not be regarded as invalidating the ceremony.

From Thailand this century Brahmavamso passes, perhaps with a sigh of relief, to 17th Century Siam.

Even in the past it is highly unlikely that a significant proportion of the bhikkhus were 'sham monks': in 17th Century Siam '… if a monk is discovered having an affair with a woman, the law condemns him to be roasted alive over a slow fire. When I was in Siam this harsh sentence was carried out on two wretches who had been convicted of this crime.' (From 'the Natural and Practical History of the Kingdom of Siam' by Nicolas Gervaise 1688, translated by John Villiers, Bangkok 1989, p 148f.) Not many bhikkhus would be game to risk such a fate, being fired from the Sangha, so to speak.

During the last three hundred years there would have been additional opportunities for breaches in the continuity of technically valid bhikkhu ordination (assuming this to have been still in existence at the beginning of the period). It therefore is obvious that in the past it was less unlikely that bhikkhu ordinations failed for lack of a quorum in 17th Century Siam than in Thailand this century. But only less *unlikely*. That it is 'highly unlikely' that in the past a significant proportion of the bhikkhus were 'sham monks' is itself highly unlikely, especially in view of the difficulty of knowing, not only whether all those conferring the ordination were really bhikkhus, but also whether the ceremony had been conducted in strict accordance with the Vinaya. The quotation from Nicolas Gervaise makes horrifying reading. According to the Vinaya, the 'punishment' for a monk who breaks the first pārājika by having sexual intercourse with a woman is immediate and automatic return to the status of layman. There is no other (religious) penalty. In 17th Century Siam, however, the law condemned him to be roasted alive over a slow fire, a sentence which the presumably Christian Gervaise characterizes as 'harsh'. One can only speculate how, in an ostensibly Buddhist country, such a barbarous and un-Buddhistic punishment came to be decreed for such an offence, and it would be interesting to know when it was last inflicted. Brahmavamso seems to think the awfulness of the punishment acted as a deterrent, so that, as fewer monks were tempted to break the first pārājika, in the past it was more than likely that bhikkhu ordination did not fail for lack of a quorum. It is no less possible, of course, that in 17th Century Siam so many bhikkhus were guilty of breaking the first pārājika that in the end the lay authorities took draconian measures to stop the rot! But why should they have done this? Why should the punishment for a breach of the Vinaya, however serious, have been characterized by such extreme cruelty? The answer is probably to be found in section IV of *Forty-Three Years Ago*, where I explain that should Theravādin lay people come to know that a bhikkhu has been guilty of a breach of the sikkhāpadas they will feel disappointed, even angry. 'They will feel disappointed not so much on account of the breach itself as because of what it means, namely, that the bhikkhu is not really a bhikkhu—and money spent supporting one who is not a bhikkhu does not make merit. It is money wasted.'[9] Thus it is not inconceivable that a medieval Siamese king, incensed by the discovery that he had been cheated out of the merit he supposed himself to have earned by the lavish support of bhikkhus who, having broken the first pārājika, were in fact not really bhikkhus, should not only have roasted the guilty parties alive over a slow fire but also have decreed that such, in future, would be the fate of any member of the Monastic Order who had an affair with a woman.

The idea of an unchaste bhikkhu being roasted alive over a slow fire Brahmavamso, it is to be noted, seems to find amusing, jocularly describing it as 'being fired from the Sangha'. The first time I saw the phrase I could hardly believe that a bhikkhu, or in fact any Buddhist, could be so insensitive as actually to make, on one of the most agonizing deaths imaginable, a silly schoolboy joke that is all too reminiscent of Mme Nhu's infamous quip about (Vietnamese) Buddhist monks 'barbecuing' themselves. Some may object that I am making too much of what is really no more than a careless phrase, but I do not think the matter can be dismissed so lightly. Since the publication of Freud's *Jokes and their Relation to the Unconscious*, as well as of his *The Psychopathology of Everyday Life*, we have become accustomed to the idea that such things as jokes, and seemingly innocent slips of the tongue, may possess a deeper significance than the person responsible for them is aware. Brahmavamso's rather perverted sense of humour suggests that there is an element of unconscious sadism in his psychological make-up or, alternatively, that his nine years as a bhikkhu in Thailand, and his preoccupation with the Vinaya, especially his concern for technically valid ordination, have had a deadening effect on his natural human feelings. Be that as it may, having made his little joke he proceeds, as he evidently believes, to bring his argument to a triumphant conclusion.

> Thus even in the past it is more than likely that bhikkhu ordinations did not fail for lack of a quorum. Indeed, there is no legitimate evidence at all to doubt the validity of the bhikkhu ordination today. To suggest otherwise is to be misinformed or simply pernicious.

Here, it is interesting to observe, Brahmavamso becomes more categorical with every sentence, even though he adduces no fresh evidence in support of his position. It is as though the mere reiteration of that position is sufficient to increase his conviction of its rightness. At first it is only 'more than likely' that bhikkhu ordinations did not fail for lack of quorum even in the past. (The 'even' suggests that ordinations were more likely to fail for lack of quorum in the past than in the present, whereas statistically the contrary is the case.) Then 'there is no legitimate evidence at all to doubt the validity of the bhikkhu ordination today,' as though from the *unlikelihood* of ordinations not failing for lack of quorum in the past it was possible to deduce the *indubitability* of valid, i.e. quorate, ordination in the present. Brahmavamso does not say what he means by 'legitimate' as distinct from illegitimate evidence. Presumably illegitimate evidence is that which gives reason for doubting the validity of bhikkhu ordination. In any case, he appears to assume that it is the invalidity of bhikkhu ordination that has to be proved rather than its validity: an assumption which—in view of the opportunities there have been, in the course of twenty-five centuries, for breaches in the continuity of technically valid bhikkhu ordination—is very much open to question. Finally, Brahmavamso declares that to suggest—even to *suggest!*— that there is any legitimate evidence to doubt the validity of the bhikkhu ordination today is to be misinformed or simply pernicious. Thus he places before me, and anyone else venturing to doubt the validity of bhikkhu ordination today, two rather unpleasant alternatives. If we are not misinformed we must be pernicious, and if we are not pernicious we must be misinformed. There is, of course, always the possibility of one's being misinformed, or inadequately informed, or of one's giving a wrong interpretation of such information as one happens to possess. But *pernicious*? According to the dictionary, pernicious means: '1. wicked and malicious. 2. Causing grave harm; deadly.' As I cannot believe that Brahmavamso means to characterize me as either wicked or malicious for doubting the validity of the bhikkhu ordination today, I assume he believes that I cause grave harm by so doing, even that I am deadly. But to what or to whom do

I cause 'grave harm', or am 'deadly'? Obviously to bhikkhu ordination, in the technical Vinaya sense, and those whose spiritual life, as bhikkhus, is based on their belief in the validity of such ordination. In his editorial, introducing Brahmavamso's article, Ajahn Khemadhammo comments that 'the Sangha, the Bhikkhu Sangha [sic!], is one amongst a number of things, such as traditional observances, methods of meditation, difficult and rather threatening teachings like that of No Self, that can really unsettle some people.' This is very true. People can certainly be unsettled, at least initially, by the idea of the (celibate) monastic life, whether Vinaya-style or Sūtra-style, by traditional observances like the Sevenfold Puja, by methods of meditation such as the Six Element Practice, and by difficult and (ego-) threatening teachings like those of No Self and the Void. But if they are Theravādins, and especially if they are bhikkhus, they can also be unsettled, it would appear, by any challenge to the validity of the bhikkhu ordination, in the technical Vinaya sense—a challenge that not only strikes at the root of the bhikkhu's spiritual and socio-religious status but also dismantles the whole machinery of 'merit-making'. As Khemadhammo goes on to observe, 'not enough is taught about kilesa (mental defilement) and the stepping back and paying attention to the effect that things have on one's mind.' Did Brahmavamso, I wonder, (or Khemadhammo himself, for that matter) step back and pay attention to the effect that *Forty-Three Years Ago* was having on his mind? Did he ask himself why the booklet had, as it would appear, 'unsettled' him, and why he felt compelled to reply to it in the way he did? In writing my 'Reflections on my Bhikkhu Ordination', I was concerned to explore the implications of a painful personal experience: the discovery that there had been a flaw in my ordination ceremony, that really I had not been ordained, and that technically I was not a bhikkhu. Brahmavamso is not concerned with this experience of mine, or what it might have meant for me, and he refers to it just in passing. Nor is he concerned with the true nature of ordination (*saṁvara*), with the difference between Vinaya- and Sūtra-style monasticism, with the negative effect on bhikkhus of the extreme veneration shown them by the Theravādin laity, with the plight of the maejes, or with any of the other important topics discussed in *Forty-Three Years Ago*. His sole concern is to safeguard the spiritual and socio-religious status of the bhikkhu by vindicating the validity, in the technical Vinaya sense, of the bhikkhu ordination today.

Having done this, at least in his own estimation, Brahmavamso proceeds to deal, briefly, with the *meaning* of Theravāda bhikkhu ordination.

Enough has been said by me now on the technicalities of Vinaya which do in fact prove the validity of the Theravada bhikkhu ordination, what now of its meaning? First it is worth emphasizing that no lay-scholar, nor part-time bhikkhu, can ever fathom the profundity of the bhikkhu ordination. They would be like someone on the outside peering through the window of a house thinking they can understand what goes on inside—the reality is that they miss too much. Only a bhikkhu of many years who has lived the lifestyle in a traditional context can ever really know the meaning of the bhikkhu ordination. You have to bite the mango to realise the taste.

Brahmavamso has indeed said a lot on the technicalities of Vinaya, even if not really enough to prove the validity of the Theravāda bhikkhu ordination, and it is not surprising that he should not want to leave us with the impression that Vinaya is simply a matter of technicalities. Hence the rather rhetorical 'what now of its meaning?' But what does he *mean* by 'meaning'? (The meaning of meaning has been the subject of much philosophical discussion, especially in the present century.) He does not say. Neither does he actually tell us what the 'meaning' of Vinaya is. He only tells us that the non-bhikkhu cannot know that meaning or, what apparently amounts to the same thing, cannot ever fathom the profundity of the bhikkhu ordination. There is, of course, an element of truth in this. The non-bhikkhu can no more know the meaning of bhikkhu ordination, in the sense of knowing what it is really like to live the traditional bhikkhu life for a long period of time, than the non-parent can know the meaning of parenthood, the non-artist the meaning of art (in the sense of creative activity), or the non-lover the meaning of love. These are all instances of the radical difference between subjective knowledge, in the sense of the knowledge a person has of himself *ab intra*, and objective knowledge, in the sense of the knowledge a person has of another person (or of a thing) *ab extra*, and there is in principle no more—and perhaps no less—reason to speak of the 'profundity' of the bhikkhu ordination than there is to speak of the profundity of parenthood, art, love, and so on. All personal experience, qua personal experience, is opaque to objective knowledge.

But Brahmavamso is not simply maintaining that one has to live as a bhikkhu in order to know what it means to live as a bhikkhu. By a kind of semantic sleight of hand he tries to maintain that one has to live as a bhikkhu in order to know that the bhikkhu ordination, in the technical Vinaya sense, is valid. Put in logical form, his argument would run: Personal experience is not accessible to objective knowledge. The meaning of the bhikkhu life is a matter of personal experience. Therefore the bhikkhu ordination, in the technical Vinaya sense, is valid today. What Brahmavamso overlooks, or ignores, or does not care to recognize, is that the technical validity of bhikkhu ordination is not a matter of personal experience. It is something that belongs to the sphere of objective knowledge, and the fact of its so belonging is not to be disguised by attempting to cloak bhikkhu ordination, in the technical Vinaya sense, in the 'profundity' that properly pertains to the living of the bhikkhu life, even as it pertains to all other forms of personal experience. Brahmavamso is indeed tacitly operating with two different meanings of the 'meaning' of bhikkhu ordination, and switches from one to the other without warning. One meaning is that of the actual experience of living the bhikkhu life. The other is the fact of one's being a bhikkhu, in the technical Vinaya sense. Contrary to what he seems to believe, or to want us to believe, what is true of bhikkhu ordination understood in the first sense, i.e. that such ordination, being a matter of personal experience, is inaccessible to objective knowledge, is by no means true of bhikkhu ordination understood in the second sense. Brahmavamso is able to make what is true of the one appear true of the other only by omitting to distinguish between the two different meanings of 'bhikkhu ordination' and then employing them indiscriminately, which he is able to do because he does not tell us what he *means* by 'meaning', or by Vinaya and bhikkhu ordination, in the first place.

The two comparisons with which he seeks to clinch his argument are therefore beside the point, and serve only to underline its fallaciousness. Someone on the outside peering through the window of a house obviously cannot understand what goes on inside, but they certainly can see whether the window frame is rotten or whether there is a hole in the ceiling. Bhikkhu ordination in the sense of the living of the bhikkhu life corresponds to what goes on inside the house. It is inaccessible to objective knowledge, being a matter of personal experience. Bhikkhu ordination in the technical Vinaya sense corresponds to the house, or to part of the house. Not only is it accessible (in theory) to objective knowledge; it is not accessible in any other way, i.e. it cannot be a matter of personal experience. Similarly with the other comparison. You have to bite the mango to realize the taste because taste is a matter of personal experience. The technical validity of your bhikkhu ordination, however, is not something that can be experienced, so there is no question of your being able to 'realize', by means of personal experience, that you are validly ordained. What you *can* experience and realize are such things as your going for Refuge to the Three Jewels, your observance of the sikkhāpadas, and your stepping back and paying attention to the effect that things have on your mind—and surely that is a great deal!

But although you have to bite the mango to realize the taste you can, it seems, at least recognize it for a mango by seeing—and admiring—its beautiful golden skin. Brahmavamso makes the concession with the help of an ethnological concept.

Nevertheless, the bhikkhu ordination can be known by everybody as a rite of passage whereby a Buddhist man, already gone for refuge to the Triple Gem, willingly undertakes a further commitment to a way of life personally designed by the Buddha as the most conducive, in the Buddha's view, to the realisation of Supreme Enlightenment (ARAHATTA-PHALA).

Someone on the outside peering through the window of a house cannot understand what goes on inside. However, he can see that *something* is going on and though he cannot, being outside the house, know the meaning of what is going on he can see what it is that it resembles in outward appearance. Thus the bhikkhu ordination can be 'known as' a rite of passage, for this is what it resembles when looked at 'through the window'. (I am reminded here of Plato's simile of the Cave. The non-bhikkhu is no more able to know the meaning of the bhikkhu ordination than the prisoners in the cave are able to see the fire behind them. Just as the prisoners see only the shadows cast on the end of the wall by the light of the fire, so the non-bhikkhu knows the bhikkhu ordination only as a rite of passage.) The bhikkhu ordination that is known as a rite of passage is, of course, bhikkhu ordination in the sense of the actual living of the bhikkhu life, the outward appearance of which can indeed be known, even though its meaning is a matter of personal experience. Since the meaning of bhikkhu ordination in the technical Vinaya sense cannot be understood, or its profundity fathomed, by the non-bhikkhu, bhikkhu ordination in this sense is not a rite of passage and cannot be known as such. It is what 'goes on inside', which no one peering through the window can understand.

Ordination in the technical Vinaya sense, the validity of which Brahmavamso is concerned to uphold, accordingly would appear to be a thing separate and distinct from 'the way of life personally designed by the Buddha as the most conducive ... to the realization of Supreme Enlightenment', i.e. would appear to be separate and distinct from bhikkhu ordination in the sense of the actual living of the bhikkhu life. It would even appear to be separate and distinct from the acceptance of the pāṭimokkha-sīla and commitment to a life of renunciation, of which Brahmavamso goes on to speak, for these two, inasmuch as they appertain to bhikkhu ordination in the sense of the actual living of the bhikkhu life, are constitutive of what can be known as a rite of passage. As I point out in *Forty-Three Years Ago*,[10] it is ordination in the technical Vinaya sense that really makes one a bhikkhu, not the observance of the sikkhāpadas, for it is possible to observe the sikkhāpadas without thereby being a bhikkhu. Thus to Theravādins, as to all upholders of Vinaya-style monasticism, the validity of bhikkhu ordination in the technical Vinaya sense is crucial. It therefore is to be defended at all costs, and one way of defending it is to make it a matter of personal experience by removing it from the sphere of objective knowledge, where it really belongs, and surrounding it with a mystic aura of 'profundity'.

But I must allow Brahmavamso to continue.

It is the acceptance of the Patimokkha-Sila, the rules for bhikkhus laid down by the Buddha in the Vinaya-Pitaka, which is the outward sign of the bhikkhu ordination [i.e. the bhikkhu ordination as known as a rite of passage, about which Brahmavamso is still speaking] (wearing a brown robe and never lay clothes is one of these rules), and it is the inner commitment to a life of renunciation (of the pleasures based on the five senses) which forms the internal meaning of the bhikkhu ordination.

In principle all this is common to both Vinaya-style and Sūtra-style monasticism. Both accept rules, though the number may vary and though Sūtra-style monasticism places more emphasis on the spirit than on the letter of their observance, and both are committed to a life of renunciation. Such acceptance and commitment are the outward sign and the internal meaning, respectively, of bhikkhu ordination not in the technical Vinaya sense but in the sense of the actual living of the bhikkhu life. The ordinations of both Vinaya-style and Sūtra-style monasticism can, therefore, be known as rites of passage. Both are separate and distinct from ordination in the technical Vinaya sense, even as ordination in this sense is separate and distinct from them. One who has received Vinaya-style ordination may, of course, *believe* himself to be ordained in the technical Vinaya sense (he cannot know this objectively) and may base his spiritual life as a bhikkhu and his socio-religious status on this belief, but that is a different matter. In the case of Sūtra-style monasticism, as described in section VIII of *Forty-Three Years Ago*, the monk (or FWBO anagārika) bases his observance of the additional 'monastic' precepts on his personal experience of going for Refuge to the Three Jewels, whether effective or real. His observance of those precepts, like his observance of the precepts common to all Buddhists regardless of life-style, in fact is an expression of that going for Refuge, as well as being a support for the continual deepening of his experience of the act of going for Refuge itself.

But though conceding that the bhikkhu ordination can be known as a rite of passage, Brahmavamso is far from

abandoning his conviction that the *meaning* of bhikkhu ordination can be understood only by a bhikkhu, i.e. by one
validly ordained, in the technical Vinaya sense, and to this
theme he now, in effect, returns. He returns to it, however,
without mentioning—perhaps without even noticing—that
while still speaking of 'bhikkhu ordination' he is in fact no
longer speaking of it as a rite of passage.

It is not surprising that the bhikkhu ordination has
been, will be, and is today, rightfully regarded with a
sense of awed inspiration by most Buddhists, because
it was established by the Buddha who was himself a
bhikkhu, and because it has survived unchanged in
whatever country it has gone to for over two
thousand, five hundred years or so. Something which
lasted so very long, something established by the
Buddha, something praised by the Arahats of today
and the past, SURELY IS DESERVING OF RESPECT!

The bhikkhu ordination spoken of in this passage is, of
course, bhikkhu ordination in the technical Vinaya sense.
What Brahmavamso has done is to switch from one meaning
of 'bhikkhu ordination' to another, and the fact that, having
made the switch, he proceeds to wax rhetorical and speak of
bhikkhu ordination in the technical Vinaya sense in such
glowing terms means that the assertions he makes in this
connection will have to be examined with particular care.
There are six assertions: (i) Bhikkhu ordination (of course in
the technical Vinaya sense) is regarded with awed inspiration by most Buddhists. (ii) Bhikkhu ordination was established by the Buddha. (iii) The Buddha was a bhikkhu. (iv)
The bhikkhu ordination has survived unchanged for over

two thousand, five hundred years or so. (v) What has survived so long is deserving of respect. (vi) Bhikkhu ordination is and was praised by the Arahats. I shall comment briefly on each of these assertions, which bring Brahmavamso's short article very nearly to a close.

(i) *Bhikkhu ordination* (in the technical Vinaya sense) *is regarded with awed inspiration by most Buddhists.* The phrase 'awed inspiration' is a highly expressive one, and I cannot help wishing, as Oscar Wilde is said to have wished in connection with a saying of James McNeill Whistler, that I had thought of it myself. To be awed is to experience overwhelming wonder, admiration, respect, and dread. It is the kind of emotion we feel when confronted by natural phenomena such as the Himalayas, Niagara Falls, the 'deep and dark blue ocean', and the starry midnight sky,—by human artistic achievements such as the Parthenon, the ceiling of the Sistine Chapel, and Mozart's final symphonies,—by acts of supreme moral heroism and by religious images such as those of the Burning Bush, the Last Judgement, Arjuna's 'Vision of the Universal Form' (in the *Bhagavad-gīta*), and the prophet of Islam's Night Journey through the heavens to the Throne of God. Inspiration is the state of being stimulated or aroused in one's mind, feelings, etc., to unusual activity or creativity. One is stimulated or aroused by the divine, by God or the gods, and the inspired act or creation partakes of the divinity of its source ('It came from above!' declared Handel of *Messiah*, while Dante's *Commedia* came to be styled 'Divina'). When inspired one may feel carried out of oneself, or above oneself, or may even feel that one is possessed. Nietzsche's description of inspiration in this extreme sense is well known. 'Awed inspiration' thus is the attitude of overwhelming wonder, admiration, respect, and dread one experiences in relation to the divine, or to a being of the divine order, as a result of which one is stimulated or aroused to unusual activity or creativity. According to Brahmavamso this is the attitude with which most Buddhists regard—and rightfully regard—technically valid bhikkhu ordination. Such ordination does not, of course, exist in the abstract; it exists, and can only exist, in the concrete, as embodied in the persons of ordained Buddhist men, i.e. bhikkhus. What Brahmavamso is really saying, therefore, is that most Buddhists regard—and *rightfully* regard—validly ordained bhikkhus with an attitude of awed inspiration.

Whether this is actually the case is extremely doubtful. Japan is a (predominantly) Buddhist country, but the vast majority of Japanese Buddhists, far from regarding valid bhikkhu ordination with feelings of awed inspiration have probably never heard of such a thing and never seen a validly ordained bhikkhu (except perhaps on TV). Even in China, Korea, and Tibet, and other parts of the Mahāyāna Buddhist world, where non-Theravāda (Sarvāstivāda and Dharmagūpta) Vinaya-style monasticism is well known, the fact that monks also receive Bodhisattva ordination and that monastic life itself is lived in accordance with the spirit of the Bodhisattva Ideal means that bhikshu ordination does not possess the significance it possesses for Theravāda. (In Tibet whatever awed inspiration may be felt is directed towards the tulkus or 'incarnate lamas'.) This leaves us with the Buddhists of south-east Asia, not all of whom continue to show bhikkhus the kind of veneration described in section VI of *Forty-Three Years Ago*. A Thai Buddhist scholar indeed goes so far as to characterize many Thai bhikkhus as 'simply uneducated farmers in yellow robes', a characterization hardly redolent of awed inspiration.[11] The fact is that however appropriate it may be to regard spiritual giants like Milarepa, Yuan Chwang, and Dogen, and even figures like Michaelangelo and Beethoven, with an attitude of awed inspiration, it is ludicrously inappropriate to regard in this way one who just happens to have been ordained in the technical Vinaya sense. Even if he is a good monk, his being accorded what amounts to godlike status will, in any case, almost certainly have a deleterious effect on his mind.

(ii) *Bhikkhu ordination was established by the Buddha.* The Buddha established a sangha or spiritual community, acceptance into which was marked by a rite of passage. At first that rite was very simple. The Buddha said 'Come, bhikkhu, live the spiritual life (*brahmacariya*) for the sake of the utter cessation of suffering,' whereupon the man thus addressed, whether homeless wanderer or householder, became a member of the community and 'ordained'. Subsequently the rite became more elaborate, especially after the Buddha had entrusted the bhikkhus with the responsibility for accepting new members and conferring 'ordination', which they initially did by getting the candidate to shave off the hair of head and face, don yellow 'robes', and solemnly declare that he went for Refuge to the Buddha, the Dharma, and the Sangha. Exactly at what point in the history of the Order the bhikkhu ordination ceremony assumed its final and most elaborate form, as preserved (along with 'fossil' traces of the earlier forms) in the Vinaya-Piṭaka, in the present state of our knowledge we cannot say; but it must have been after the parinirvāṇa, so that it is quite incorrect to speak of bhikkhu ordination *in that sense* as having been established by the Buddha.

(iii) *The Buddha was a bhikkhu*. An Indian friend of mine who regarded himself as a follower of the Buddha but not (he was at pains to insist) as a Buddhist, once remarked to me that although the Buddha is represented, in the Pāli scriptures, as more than once describing himself as a brahmin, he is never represented as describing himself as a bhikkhu. While one would need to have a very extensive acquaintance with the Pāli scriptures to be sure that the Buddha *never* described himself as a bhikkhu, even a limited acquaintance with them is enough to show that he was generally known, to friend and foe alike, as Samaṇa Gotama. Indeed the idea of the Enlightened One's being known as 'Bhikkhu Gotama' seems faintly absurd. To disciples like Sāriputta he was the Mahā-Samaṇa or *'Great* Samaṇa', a samaṇa, literally a '(spiritual) labourer', being a respected homeless, wandering, 'heterodox' *religieux*. If the Buddha was a bhikkhu at all he must have been a Sūtra-style bhikkhu, not a Vinaya-style one, for to be a Vinaya-style bhikkhu he would have to have been ordained, in the technical Vinaya sense, and he could hardly have been ordained, in this sense, before the Vinaya came into existence, and there is no evidence for his having been 'ordained' afterwards.

That Brahmavamso should want to see the Buddha as a bhikkhu, in the technical Vinaya sense, is perhaps indicative of his whole outlook on Buddhism, the spiritual life, and monasticism. He wants to see the Buddha as a bhikkhu, in the technical Vinaya sense, because he is an upholder of the technical validity of bhikkhu ordination in Theravāda, and therefore seeks to buttress his case by arguing that such ordination was both established by the Buddha and ex-emplified by him in his own person. I am reminded of those Thai Buddhist paintings in which the Buddha, as well as his monk disciples, is depicted looking exactly like a Thai bhik-khu, complete with neatly laundered yellow robes and a shoulder bag, the only difference being that the Buddha is shown with an uṣṇīṣa or 'cranial protuberance'. Just as theists tend to anthropomorphize the deity so, it would appear, Theravāda bhikkhus tend to 'bhikkhu-ize' the Buddha. In this connection I would like to invite Brahma-vamso's attention to an interesting passage in the *Mahā-parinibbāṇa-sutta* in which the Buddha describes to Ānanda how, before entering each of the eight 'assemblies'—of the nobles, of the brahmins, of the householders, of the samaṇas, and of the four different kinds of gods—he adopts their (distinctive) appearance and speech, whatever it might be.[12] The passage is interesting on a number of counts. It is not simply that people—or beings—experience the Buddha as one of themselves: the Buddha actually transforms himself into their likeness. More interestingly still, though he trans-forms himself into a samaṇa to communicate with samaṇas, and even into a householder to communicate with householders, he does *not* transform himself into a bhikkhu to communicate with bhikkhus. Could it be, not only that the Buddha was not a bhikkhu but that, at the time of his describing to Ānanda his mode of entering the eight assem-blies (which he may not have done immediately prior to his parinirvāṇa, the *Mahā-parinibbāṇa-sutta* being a very com-posite work) there were no bhikkhus, at least not in the technical Vinaya sense, and that even if there were bhikkhus they were subsumed under the samaṇas?

(iv) *The bhikkhu ordination has survived unchanged for over two thousand, five hundred years or so.* Monasticism is certainly a permanent feature of most forms of Buddhism. Whether there has been an uninterrupted transmission of technically valid bhikkhu ordination, in the Theravāda or any other sect or school, is quite another matter. That it is highly unlikely that there has been such a transmission, that even if there had been we could not know it, and that a spiritual life based on the *belief* that there has been one therefore rests on a very insecure foundation, is the leitmotiv running through *Forty-Three Years Ago*, and there is no need for me to repeat myself here. I refer anyone who still thinks that bhikkhu ordination has survived unchanged through the centuries to S. Dutt's *Early Buddhist Monachism*, which I have already mentioned, as well as to its successor volumes *The Buddha and Five After Centuries* and *Buddhist Monks and Monasteries of India*.

(v) *What has survived so long is deserving of respect.* Not necessarily. Evil ideas, institutions, and practices have sometimes survived for centuries, as a glance at world history will show, and these are certainly not deserving of respect. In any case did not the Buddha advise the Kālamas of Kesaputta not to go by hearsay, nor by what was handed down by others, nor by what people said, nor by what was stated on the authority of their traditional teachings? Such advice as this is not suggestive of respect for mere antiquity.

(vi) *Bhikkhu ordination is and was praised by the Arahats.* Arahats are those who have realized Supreme Enlightenment (*arahata-phala*). While such exalted beings will certainly praise the spiritual life (*brahmacariya*), and even praise Sūtra-style monasticism, I for one find it difficult to imagine them praising bhikkhu ordination, in the technical Vinaya sense, as such, and it is ordination *in this sense* that Brahmavamso considers important, which he believes he and other bhikkhus possess, for the validity of which he is arguing, and of which, finally, he declares 'it SURELY IS DESERVING OF RESPECT!'

The concluding paragraph of Brahmavamso's article strikes an apologetic, even a defensive, note.

> In this article I have not meant to compare the
> bhikkhu ordination with any other rite of passage into
> any other order, nor to praise one group (the Bhikkhu
> Sangha) by putting down another group. I have
> written this article only to defend the validity and
> meaning of the Bhikkhu Ordination, and thereby to
> defend [a Freudian slip for 'attack' or 'rebut'?] the
> challenge to the integrity of the Theravada
> Bhikkhu-Sangha. May all Buddhists grow and prosper
> according to the Dhamma, whether bhikkhu or
> otherwise.

I am sure we can accepts the writer's protestation that in his article he has not meant to compare the bhikkhu ordination with any other rite of passage into any other order. Not that it might not be instructive to compare such rites of passage, provided the intention was not invidious, and it is presumably his meaning to compare them invidiously that Brahmavamso really is disclaiming. But though he may not mean to praise one group, the Bhikkhu Sangha, at the expense of another, this is what in effect he does and, given his fundamental position, cannot help doing. The Bhikkhu Sangha is the community of the validly ordained. It is the community of those who have received that ordination—in the technical Vinaya sense—which, according to Brahmavamso, is rightfully the object of 'awed inspiration' to all Buddhists, and who, as embodiments of that ordination, are in practice themselves rightly regarded with awed inspiration. Bhikkhu ordination, in the technical Vinaya sense, is even praised by the Arahats, the Supremely Enlightened—a praise obviously implying praise of the recipients of the ordination, apart from whom such a thing as 'ordination' cannot exist. Non-bhikkhus, however spiritually developed, are not objects of awed inspiration. They are not praised by the Arahats. It is therefore difficult to see how Brahmavamso can honestly claim that in praising one group, the Bhikkhu Sangha, he is not putting down another group, i.e. a group whose members are not bhikkhus, whether they are Jodo Shin Shu 'priests', Tantric lay yogins and yoginis, or even Dharmacharis and Dharmacharinis of the Western Buddhist Order. Surely all those who practise the Dharma to a superlative degree, whether living as monks or nuns, or as laymen or laywomen, or in any other way, are worthy of being regarded with awed inspiration! Surely the Arahats—and Bodhisattvas—will praise them unreservedly! Surely they will praise all those who go for Refuge—even if only 'effectively', as we say in the FWBO—in the knowledge that such have taken hold of the end of a golden string which, if they only can wind it into a ball, will lead them in at one or another of the three Gates of Liberation, built in the wall of the city of Nirvāṇa!

What we really need to defend is not technicalities of the Vinaya, or the validity and meaning of bhikkhu ordination, but the fundamental principles of Buddhism and the significance and value of the spiritual life (*brahmacariya*), both of which are currently under attack from so many quarters. What we need to defend is the integrity of the Dharma as the principial path to Supreme Enlightenment. If we can do *that* then all Buddhists, i.e. all who genuinely go for Refuge to the Three Jewels, in whatever degree, will indeed grow and prosper according to the Dharma. What is more, they will be in a position to help others grow and prosper according to the Dharma too.

Notes and References

1 Sangharakshita, *Forty-Three Years Ago: Reflections on my Bhikkhu Ordination, on the Occasion of the Twenty-Fifth Anniversary of the Western Buddhist Order.* Windhorse, Glasgow 1993, p.25.

2 Sangharakshita, op. cit. p.11.

3 Trans. I.B. Horner, *The Book of the Discipline* (Vinaya-Pitaka), vol.iv, Pali Text Society, London 1951, pp.458–9.

4 *Dhammapada* vv.360–382. Trans. A.P. Buddhadatta Mahāthera, *Dhammapadaṁ. An Anthology of the Sayings of the Buddha,* Colombo (no date), pp.96–102.

5 Sangharakshita, op. cit. p.42.

6 Sangharakshita, op. cit. p.25 et seq.

7 Sangharakshita, op. cit. p.22.

8 Readers of *Facing Mount Kanchenjunga* may recall that at my bhikkhu ordination in India in 1950 there was present a Ladakhi 'incarnate lama', Kusho Bakula. As he belonged to a non-Theravāda line of monastic ordination he sat outside the sīmā. According to Brahmavamso, he could have sat inside the sīmā and even acted as my preceptor.

9   Sangharakshita, op. cit. p.27.

10 Sangharakshita, op. cit. p.24.

11 Chatsumarn Kabilsingh, *Thai Women in Buddhism*, Parallax, Berkeley 1991, p.83.

12 *Dīgha-Nikāya* XVI. 3.21–3.

The Windhorse symbolizes the energy of the enlightened mind carrying the Three Jewels —the Buddha, the Dharma, and the Sangha—to all sentient beings.

Buddhism is one of the fastest growing spiritual traditions in the Western world. Throughout its 2,500-year history, it has always succeeded in adapting its mode of expression to suit whatever culture it has encountered.

Windhorse Publications aims to continue this tradition as Buddhism comes to the West. Today's Westerners are heirs to the entire Buddhist tradition, free to draw instruction and inspiration from all the many schools and branches. Windhorse publishes works by authors who not only understand the Buddhist tradition but are also familiar with Western culture and the Western mind.

For orders and catalogues contact

WINDHORSE PUBLICATIONS	ARYALOKA
UNIT 1-316	HEARTWOOD CIRCLE
THE CUSTARD FACTORY	NEWMARKET
GIBB STREET	NEW HAMPSHIRE
BIRMINGHAM B9 4AA	NH 03857
UK	USA

Windhorse Publications is an arm of the Friends of the Western Buddhist Order, which has more than forty centres on four continents. Through these centres, members of the Western Buddhist Order offer regular programmes of events for the general public and for more experienced students. These include meditation classes, public talks, study on Buddhist themes and texts, and 'bodywork' classes such as t'ai chi, yoga, and massage. The FWBO also runs several retreat centres and the Karuna Trust, a fundraising charity that supports social welfare projects in the slums and villages of India.

Many FWBO centres have residential spiritual communities and ethical businesses associated with them. Arts activities are encouraged too, as is the development of strong bonds of friendship between people who share the same ideals. In this way the FWBO is developing a unique approach to Buddhism, not simply as a set of techniques, less still as an exotic cultural interest, but as a creatively directed way of life for people living in the modern world.

If you would like more information about the FWBO please write to

LONDON BUDDHIST CENTRE
51 ROMAN ROAD
LONDON
E2 OHU
UK

ARYALOKA
HEARTWOOD CIRCLE
NEWMARKET
NEW HAMPSHIRE
NH 03857
USA

ALSO FROM WINDHORSE

SANGHARAKSHITA

A SURVEY OF BUDDHISM

Now in its seventh edition, *A Survey of Buddhism* continues to provide an indispensable study of the entire field of Buddhist thought and practice. Covering all the major doctrines and traditions, both in relation to Buddhism as a whole and to the spiritual life of the individual Buddhist, Sangharakshita places their development in historical context. This is an objective but sympathetic appraisal of Buddhism's many forms that clearly demonstrates the underlying unity of all its schools.

'It would be difficult to find a single book in which the history and development of Buddhist thought has been described as vividly and clearly as in this survey. ... For all those who wish to "know the heart, the essence of Buddhism as an integrated whole", there can be no better guide than this book.' *Lama Anagarika Govinda*

'I recommend Sangharakshita's book as the best survey of Buddhism.' *Dr Edward Conze*

544 pages, Bibliography, Index,
Paperback £12.99/$24.95
ISBN 0 904776 65 9

SANGHARAKSHITA

THE HISTORY OF MY GOING FOR REFUGE

The founder of the Western Buddhist Order traces the 'erratic
process of discovery' that has led him to conclude that the
monastic life-style and spiritual life are not identical, that it is
possible to be a good monk or nun and at the same time a bad
Buddhist, and that the Going for Refuge—the act of commitment
to Buddhist spiritual ideals—is the central and definitive act of
the Buddhist life, and the fundamental basis of unity among
Buddhists.

For anyone concerned with the spiritual vitality of the Buddhist
tradition—and with its transmission in the modern world—this
meticulously plotted 'History' makes indispensable reading.

130 pages
Paperback £4.95/$9.95
ISBN 0 904766 33 0